BIRMINGHA
BACK TO THE
SIXTIES

Alton & Jo Douglas

The Green, Erdington, 17th January 1963.

© 2004 Alton and Jo Douglas
ISBN 1 85858 258 X
Published by Brewin Books Ltd., Doric House, 56 Alcester Road, Studley, Warwickshire B80 7LG.
Printed by Warwick Printing Co. Ltd., Caswell Road, Leamington Spa, Warwickshire CV31 1QD.
Layout by Alton and Jo Douglas

Kingstanding Road, Perry Barr, 8th February 1967.

Front Cover: The Market Hall stands in defiant isolation, as the Bull Ring redevelopment is underway, 25th April 1961.

C o n t e n t s

BREWIN BOOKS LTD

Doric House, 56 Alcester Road,
Studley, Warwickshire B80 7LG

Tel: 01527 854228 Fax: 01527 852746

Vat Registration No. 705 0077 73

Dear Nostalgic,

Do you remember that mesmerising moment in Hitchcock's classic film, "The Lady Vanishes", when Miss Froy's handwriting disappears from the window of the train? Each time I see it I think about our books and it brings a sense of urgency to every project. Well, Miss Froy would have been proud of the permanency of this collection – literally, hundreds of treasures preserved for all time – shops by the basketful, enough events to fill a decade of diaries, famous names from the past remembered forever. Enjoy the sixties, we did then and now we can again.

Yours, in friendship,

Alton

The Lord Mayor and Lady Mayoress, Alderman and Mrs James Meadows, talk to cast members from "Crossroads", Noele Gordon, Susan Hanson and Sue Nichols, ATV's Alpha Studios, Aston, 4th April 1968.

1960

Alcester Road South, Kings Heath, 15th January 1960.

Bull Ring, c 1960.

Somerset Road, Handsworth, 10th March 1960.

Crompton Road, Handsworth, March 1960.

Councillor Denis Thomas, Chairman of the Public Works Committee,
switches on the lights on the newly-opened section of the inner ring road,
11th March 1960.

At a dance, to commemorate the coming of age of the Stonehouse Gang, some of the original members practise the
art of mime. The club's founder, Harry Webb, plays the role of conductor, 26th March 1960.

Alum Rock Road, 5th April 1960.

Stratford Road, Sparkhill, 2nd May 1960.

Recording "From the English Midlands" for BBC World Service, BBC, Broad Street, 1960.

Keith Ackrill interviews Hungarian film star, Eva Bartok, for Birmingham Hospitals' Broadcasting, May 1960. She was here to promote her autobiography, "Worth Living For" and the film, "Operation Amsterdam".

Waiting to take part in Cromwell Hall's Anniversary Parade, Heath Green Road, Winson Green, June 1960.

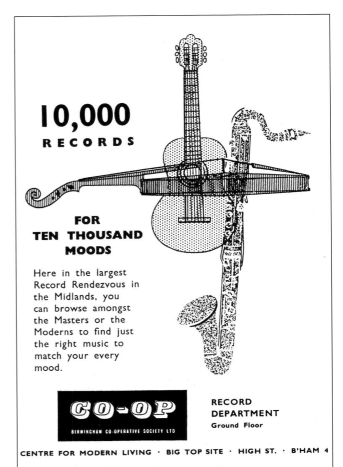
8

Lionel Street/Snow Hill, 1960.

A toast to the last day of the old Scala cinema, Smallbrook Street, 4th June 1960.

Oxford Road/Warwick Road, Acocks Green, 2nd September 1960.

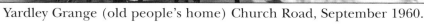

Yardley Grange (old people's home) Church Road, September 1960.

John Bright Street/Navigation Street, 21st September 1960.

Chester Road, Erdington, 5th October 1960.

Villa Road, Handsworth, 12th December 1960.

Bull Street, with Dr Johnson Passage on the left, 1960.

Alexandra Theatre

EVENINGS at 7-0   MATINEES at 2.30
(Boxing Day at 2 p.m)

COMMENCING CHRISTMAS EVE AT 7-0

DEREK SALBERG presents his spectacular Comedy Pantomime

Sinbad the Sailor

GEORGE LACY   **MORECAMBE AND WISE**

LINDA LEE   **ANTON AND JANETTA MORROW**

THE FOUR PLAYBOYS   **JOHNNY STEWART**   **THREE GHEZZIS**

SYLVIA BRIAR

DEREK ROYLE   **HANS BELA and MARY**

WILLIAM AVENELL   **ARTHUR TOLCHER**

LEHMISKI LADIES   **LYNNETTE RAE**   **ROSELLI SINGERS**

1961

Installing the lights to illuminate the interior of Birmingham Cathedral, for the Festival of Sound and Light, 3rd January 1961.

Lichfield Road, Aston, 10th January 1961.

Alcester Road/Woodbridge Road, Moseley, 30th January 1961.

Rev Norman Power shows how it's done, to some of the members of
St John's Church Boys' Club, Ladywood, 5th March 1961.

The foundation stone of Stechford Baths is laid by the Lord
Mayor, Alderman Garnet Boughton, 22nd March 1961.

14

Holyhead Road, with The Albion cinema on the left, Handsworth, 21st April 1961.

York Road, Kings Heath, 26th April 1961.

Students from Sierra Leone present the Lord Mayor and Lady Mayoress, Alderman and Mrs Garnet Boughton, with their national flag, 26th April 1961.

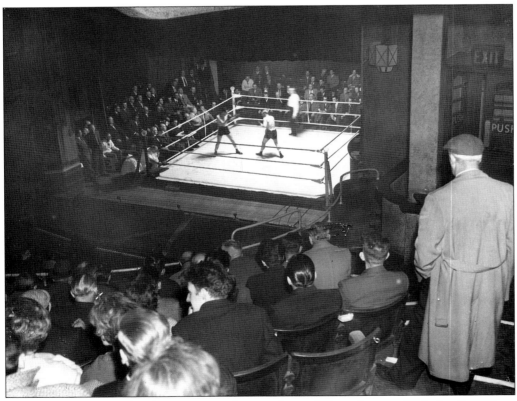

The first night of boxing presentations at Aston Hippodrome, 28th April 1961.

Leach Green Lane, Rednal, 30th May 1961.

The Lord Mayor, Alderman Eric Mole, chats with members of the Sons of Rest before they leave for their annual outing, this time to Bristol Zoo, 1961.

Great Hampton Row, with St George's Place on the left, Newtown, 18th August 1961.

Francis Street, Nechells Green, 13th September 1961.

Smallbrook Ringway, showing the underpass into Hurst Street, 1961.

19

Great Charles Street/Snow Hill, 1961.

St Martin's Bookshop, on the day of its opening, Bull Ring, 28th September 1961.

Councillor Denis Thomas cuts the tape to officially open the Camp Hill flyover, 16th October 1961.

The MP for Yardley, Leonard Cleaver, leads a triumphant party across the junction of Station Road and Bordesley Green East, 13th November 1961. It marked the end of a three year battle to get lights installed at this dangerous location.

1962

Soho Road, Handsworth, January 1962.

Councillor Charles Horton (right), Chairman of the Midland Museum Service and Derek Dooley (administrator), prepare some items that will form part of the travelling exhibition which is touring the Midlands, 30th January 1962.

A LEW PHILLIPS PROMOTION

TUESDAY, FEBRUARY 27th, 1962

EMBASSY SPORTSDROME

FIGHTS

15 x 3 min. rounds Contest for the FLYWEIGHT CHAMPIONSHIP OF GT. BRITAIN at 8 st.

BRIAN CARTWRIGHT   versus   **JACKIE BROWN**
(Birmingham)   (Edinburgh)

12 x 3 min. rounds Contest MIDLAND AREA HEAVYWEIGHT TITLE

JOHNNY PRESCOTT   versus   **JACK WHITTAKER**
(Birmingham) Holder   (Warwick) Challenger

10 rounds WELTERWEIGHT CONTEST at 10st. 9lbs.

WALLY SWIFT   versus   **SAMMY COWAN**
(Nottingham)   (Belfast)

8 rounds LIGHTWEIGHT CONTEST at 9st. 12lbs.

TERRY EDWARDS   versus   **JOHN JARRETT**
(Smethwick)   (Belfast)

8 rounds MIDDLEWEIGHT CONTEST at 11st. 8lbs.

WILLIE FISHER   versus   **JULIUS CAESAR**
(Craigneuk)   (Rhodesia)

6 x 3 min. rounds MIDDLEWEIGHT CONTEST at 11st. 8lbs.

SID BROWN   versus   **TEDDY GARDNER**
(Birmingham)   (Croydon)

6 rounds CONTEST at 10st. 12lbs.

TERRY BANNING   versus   **STEVE GIBSON**
(Leamington)   (Derby)

OFFICIALS:

Referees: (Appointed by B.B.B. of C.)
  Brian Cartwright v Jackie Brown: Mr. Tommy Little (London)
  Remainder of Bill: Mr. Mickey Fox and Mr. Frank Parkes

Promoter-Matchmaker: LEW PHILLIPS   Whip: SIDNEY DAY
M.C.: JOHN SPRING   Seconds: JACK MILLER and JACK POND
Timekeeper: MICK MARSH   Steward in Charge: MR. BASIL WILLIAMS
  Scales by courtesy of AVERY'S   Officials appointed by B.B.B. of C.
Medical Officer: DR. S. ROSE

Rupert Street/Oliver Street, Nechells Green, 1962.

Globe Works, Highgate Street/Upper Highgate Street, 1962.

St Jude's Church, Hill Street, 2nd March 1962. The Albany Hotel was under construction on the left and the church was demolished shortly afterwards.

New Street, 1962.

CANNING   '20' CLUB

ANNUAL DINNER

given by kind
Invitation of the Directors

★

Held at
Head Office,
Great Hampton Street,
Birmingham, 18.

★

Thursday, 15th March, 1962

BIRMINGHAM CATHEDRAL
(By kind permission of the Provost)

TUESDAY, 27th MARCH, 1962

at 7.30 p.m.

BIRMINGHAM INSURANCE CHOIR

with Orchestra
(Leader: Dennis Avery)

MASS IN G (No. 2) .... *Schubert*
ORGAN CONCERTO No. 13 IN F .... *Handel*
    (The Cuckoo and the Nightingale)

CANTATA No. 112 .... *Bach*
    (The Lord is my Shepherd)

with

ALISON MIDDLETON	JOHN SOUTHALL
(Soprano)	(Counter-Tenor)
IAN COLE	HENRY SANDON
(Tenor)	(Bass)

ROY MASSEY
(Organ)

Conductor: RAYMOND ISAACSON

———————

Admission by Programme   -   Four Shillings
Students   -   Two Shillings

Programmes may be obtained from:—
    Atlas Assurance Company Ltd., 114 Colmore Row,
    Miss Harding, Midland Employers Mutual Assurance Ltd., Midland
        Assurance Building, Hagley Road, 16,
    The Royal Insurance Company Ltd., 7 Bennett's Hill,
    Civic Radio Ltd., 1 Easy Row,
    and from members of the Choir.

The National Federation of Music Societies, to which this Society is
affiliated, supports this concert with funds provided by the Arts Council
of Great Britain.

Shard End Carnival procession, Brookmeadow Road, 1962.

Chester Road, Castle Bromwich, 26th June 1962.

The Lord Mayor, Alderman E W Horton, at the official opening of "The Circus", the new Civic Restaurant, Ringway, 2nd July 1962.

New Meeting Street, looking towards Moor Street, 19th September 1962.

Suffolk Street/Severn Street, 19th September 1962.

Rear of Milton Street, Newtown, 24th September 1962.

Lea Village, 17th October 1962.

Shane Fenton and Carol Deene compare outfits with the
conservatively dressed Matt Monro, at a recording of ABC
Television's "Thank Your Lucky Stars", Aston, 12th November 1962.

Pershore Road, Stirchley, 1962.

Pop singer, Adam Faith, (left) presents a special cake to the ABC Minors Club, (Oak Cinema, Selly Oak) at the Birmingham Hippodrome, 17th November 1962. It was then taken to the children's ward at Selly Oak Hospital.

Preparations underway for the next stage of the inner ring road, with the Old Square, bottom right, 1962.

H. JOHN DUNKERLEY, C.B.E., B.A.

President — BIRMINGHAM HOSPITALS
BROADCASTING ASSOCIATION

Invites you to the

Official Opening of the

NEW STUDIOS

by The Right Worshipful The Lord Mayor

of Birmingham - Alderman E. W. Horton, J.P.

at the Midlands Electricity Board,

Dale End, Birmingham, 4.

on Monday, November, 19th.

at 2.30 p.m.

Recording of "Trolley Service" at the Birmingham Hospitals'
Broadcasting Association Studios, Dale End, 1962. The programme was
transmitted on the Midlands' Home Service.

The Rt Hon Ernest Marples, Minister of Transport, answers questions at a Press Conference, Council Chambers,
19th November 1962. It was part of a provincial tour to explain the programme of new roads.

1963

The new Post Office television detector vehicle hits the streets of the city, 24th January 1963.

Edmund Street, from Easy Row, 30th January 1963.

Easy Row, 6th February 1963.

A swathe is cut through the grounds of St Martin's Church, as the Bull Ring alterations are underway,
7th March 1963.

Gerry Levene and the Avengers.

Danny King, one of the city's most successful exponents of Rock 'n Roll.

Denny Laine and the Diplomats.

Keith Powell and the Valets.

The Yew Tree Inn, Brookvale Road, Witton, 1963.

The Queen visits the Bull Ring Market to check on the reconstruction, 24th May 1963. Accompanying her is the Lord Mayor, Alderman Louis Glass and the Chairman of the Markets' and Fairs' Committee, Councillor Mrs N Smith.

The ever-growing Rotunda, 1963.

Denis Howell, MP for Small Heath, leads his team out in the match to raise funds for the Freedom of Hunger Campaign, Valor Sports Ground, Erdington, 14th July 1963. The actor, Ian Carmichael, can be seen (back left) and England batsman, Tom Graveney, is over Mr Howell's right shoulder.

Navigation Street/Suffolk Street, 1st August 1963.

Hill Street/Station Street, 1st August 1963.

Wyndhurst Road, Stechford, 1963.

Sherborne Road/Orchard Road, Balsall Heath, 1963.

TODAY a new Planet is born. The Papers and Publications Group of newspapers, who have already successfully opened new colour weekly newspapers in Swindon and Coventry, now launch out on one of the most exciting ventures in provincial journalism.

The full-colour Birmingham Planet will blaze a new trail. It will be a paper for the moderns. Features will be topical, and news bright and up to the minute.

When readers write in we invite them to suggest new features they would like to see in the Planet.

For the first issue, Woodrow Wyatt, M.P., chairman of the Planet, opens a series of articles on page 4, entitled "What Birmingham means to me." Other well-known writers and personalities are booked to follow.

On the sport side, Mr. Joe Mercer, the Aston Villa manager, writes on page 31. He answers critics who claim that he should go out and spend to put Villa back on the winning trail.

There is also a full-colour three-page feature on the giant British Motor Corporation works at Longbridge on pages 15-17. These are in addition to other features to suit all members of the family.

5.9.63

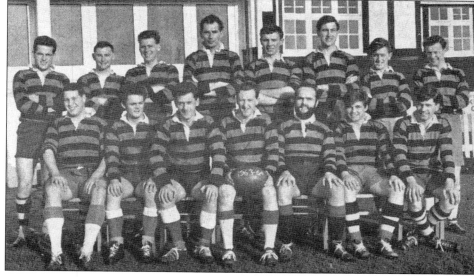

Lucas Rugby Club First XV, 1963.

"Dixon of Dock Green", one of the most popular TV programmes in the sixties, led by Jack Warner (left) as PC George Dixon.

The Chairman of the Birmingham Post and Mail, Eric Clayson (later Sir),
bowls the first ball at the new Warwick Bowl, Acocks Green,
19th September 1963.

Birmingham-born singer, David Hughes, signs photographs, after opening the Friends of Selly Oak Hospital Bazaar, 9th November 1963.

The Midland Operatic Company rehearsing for "Gay's the Word", Birmingham Hippodrome, November 1963.

Bristol Road, Selly Oak, 1963.

Edmund Street, with Big Brum just visible on the left, 30th December 1963.

Nursery Road/Villa Street, Hockley, 1964.

Frank Sinatra Jnr., in town to appear at the Odeon, New Street, with the Tommy Dorsey Orchestra, (led by Sam Donahue), January 1964.

Raddlebarn Road/Tiverton Road, Selly Oak, 1964.

Singer, Frankie Vaughan, arrives to present a car to the winner of a competition at Radwar Motors Ltd, Holyhead Road, March 1964.

The last day for crossings' officer, Cliff Warwick, at Bishop
Ryder Primary School, Gem Street, Gosta Green,
15th April 1964.

Erdington pensioners just about to leave for a conference at Scarborough, May 1964.

The Duke of Edinburgh, with the Lord Mayor, Alderman Frank Price and the City Engineer and Surveyor, Sir Herbert Manzoni, at the official opening of the new Bull Ring Centre, 29th May 1964.

Senior Citizens, from Newtown, about to leave for a day trip to London, June 1964.

G. Willetts (motor engineers), Gracemere Crescent, Hall Green, 8th June 1964.

PACKING CASE MAKERS

PERRY & CASTLE LTD.

BOXES AND CRATES
ZINC AND TIN LINING
NEW AND SECOND HAND CASES
BOX BOARDS IN SHOOK
STILLAGES

37-39 GROSVENOR STREET, WEST
LADYWOOD . . 16.

TELEPHONE: MIDLAND 7271

Winners of the Lorry Driver of the Year competition, Fort Dunlop, 1964.

Highfield Road, Hall Green, 9th June 1964.

Off for a week's holiday in Towyn, Merionethshire, for the children from Rea Street South Nursery, Digbeth, Summer 1964.

Bristol Road South, Northfield, 11th September 1964.

Edgewood Road, Rednal, 8th October 1964.

Nursery Road/Wellesley Street, Handsworth, 9th October 1964.

Birmingham entrants in the Miss GPO-Interflora Personality Girl 1964 Contest.

Church Road, Yardley, 2nd November 1964.

Quinton motorway, carving out the future, 12th November 1964.

The ladies of the Tascos team, winners of six trophies in the South West Birmingham Clubs' Darts' League, 1964.

Taylor Street/Bloomsbury Street, Nechells, November 1964.

Harborne Lane, Harborne, 18th November 1964.

The BBC panel, led by Robert Robinson (centre), watch the TV documentary, "Home for Heroes", a programme about Birmingham, 7th December 1964.

Knutsford Street, Balsall Heath, 11th December 1964.

Leopold Street, Highgate, 14th December 1964.

Washwood Heath Road, Ward End, 1965.

Whitehead Road/Albert Road, Aston. c.1965.

SIR WINSTON CHURCHILL died yesterday shortly after eight o'clock in the morning. A bulletin of 18 laconic words signalled, to the world he helped save from catastrophe, *finis*, in peace and without pain, to more than half a century's valiant, turbulent years.

25.1.65

Guests at the Midlands' TV Ball, including the actor Dermot Kelly (left) and next to him Mr and Mrs Pat Astley, the Belfry, Wishaw, 22nd January 1965. Pat was a Continuity Announcer at ATV and a long-time friend of Alton and Jo.

Dr George Thalben-Ball, gave over 900 recitals at the Town Hall, between 1949-1983.

Local beat group, the Rockin' Berries, are given a guided tour of the House of Commons by Donald Chapman, MP for Northfield, 29th March 1965.

Manzoni Gardens, this site now forms part of the new Bull Ring, 27th April 1965.

Chipperfield Road, Castle Bromwich, 27th April 1965.

Few lost in Bull Ring

CONSIDERING that there is room for 40,000 shoppers at a time in the new Bull Ring Centre it is a pointer to the native intelligence of the female "Brummie" and the adequacy of the coloured signposts that only 50 people were lost in the first week after its opening — and less than this subsequently.

WRESTLERS have played their part in the story of pop music. It was a wrestler, Paul Lincoln, known professionally as Dr. Death, who part-owned the 2 I's coffee bar in Soho: a place that gave the world Tommy Steele.

Now the heavyweight boxer, Johnny Prescott, has decided to manage Mike Sheridan and the Night Riders. They both come from Birmingham. Mr. Sheridan is a small young man of 22 with a gaunt though smiling face; Mr. Prescott is an enormous man of 26 with the right shoulders for the job. He has startling blue eyes set in an unsmiling face, and a modest line in conversation.

He is one of the few managers with a manager.

"My manager's manager," Mr. Sheridan said, "keeps telling him to smile."

"I'm a scowler," said Mr. Prescott, pleasantly enough.

Harborne Cricket Club, c 1965.

Clifford Street, looking into Furnace Lane, Lozells, 1965.

Anti-apartheid protestors outside the County Ground as Warwickshire play the South Africans, 22nd May 1965.

Councillor W Lawler investigates the living conditions of residents in Henley Street, Newtown, May 1965.

"Time Gentlemen, please!" for the White Horse, Congreve Street/Great Charles Street, 13th July 1965.

Broad Street/Easy Row, c 1965. It was originally intended that this site would house an enormous exhibition hall by 1967.

The Exchange Buildings are reduced to rubble, Stephenson Place, August 1965.

Devonshire Street, Winson Green, 1965.

The Daleks, from "Dr Who", take over Lewis's, during a
promotional visit, 3rd August 1965.

The Everly Brothers, starring in "Thank Your Lucky Stars",
ATV, 1965.

Members of the Bolshoi Ballet Company meet the Lord Mayor and Lady Mayoress, Alderman and Mrs George Corbyn Barrow, 7th September 1965. The Hippodrome was given a name change, by Moss Empires, to the Birmingham Theatre this particular year but reverted, due to public demand, to its original name in 1972.

Exeter Passage, off Holloway Head, 1965.

Court 11, William Edward Street, Balsall Heath, 1965.

Lea Village, Lea Hall, 17th December 1965.

Glebe Farm Road, 17th December 1965.

Taunton Road, with Stoney Lane at the traffic lights, Balsall Heath, 1966.

Heath Mill Lane, Bordesley, 21st February 1966.

The end of a 130-year landmark that towered over Hoskins and Sewell Ltd., High Street, Bordesley, 12th September 1966.

Porchester Street, Newtown, 26th September 1966.

The Midlands' President of the Birmingham and Midland Bookmakers' Association, Fred Stone and his wife (right), greet Mr and Mrs Robert Cannell at the annual banquet and ball, Penns Hall, Sutton Coldfiled, September 1966.

Birmingham motor trade employees march through
Brighton, 4th October 1966. They were en route to the
Labour Party Conference to protest at proposed
redundancies.

Bull's Head, Hatchett Street, Newtown,
22nd November 1966.

Part of the Bull Ring shopping centre, November 1966.

Brook Street/Newhall Street, 1966.

Pershore Road South, Kings Norton, 1966.

Patent Enamel Co. Ltd., Heeley Road, Selly Oak, 1966.

Malcolm House, Moseley Road, Moseley, 1966.

The joy of Christmas shopping, New Street/High Street, 10th December 1966.

Snow Hill, 21st December 1966.

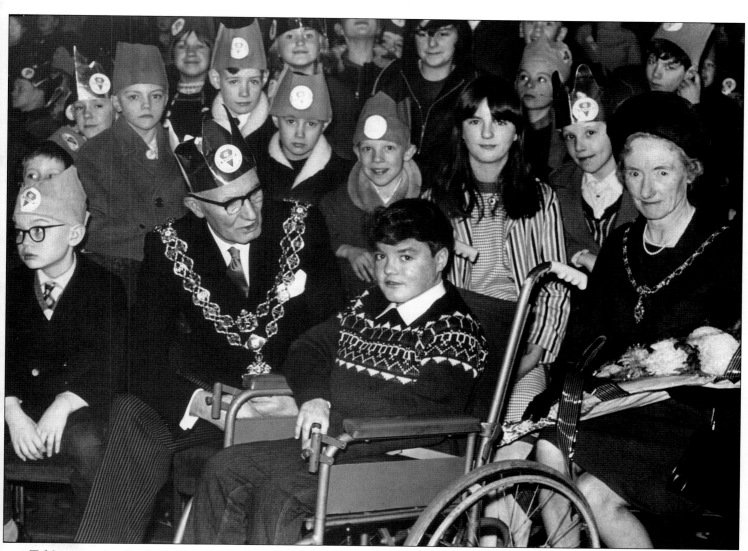

Taking part in the festivities the Lord Mayor and Lady Mayoress, Alderman and Mrs Harold Tyler, meet some of the 1400 children at the Oak Cinema, Selly Oak, 24th December 1966.

Bargain hunters at the Beehive, Albert Street, 3rd January 1967.

Harrison Road, Erdington, 1st February 1967. In the late seventies Mr Gilroy Bevan became the Conservative MP for Yardley.

Grosvenor Hotel, Hagley Road, Five Ways, 1967.

Green Lane, Small Heath, 28th February 1967.

Hospital Street/Frankfort Street, Newtown, 8th March 1967.

Bishopsgate Street/William Street, Highgate, 7th April 1967.

Waterloo vs Moseley at The Reddings, 10th April 1967.

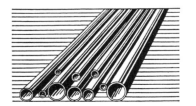

Cherrywood Road/Denbigh Street, Bordesley Green, May 1967.

Silver Street, Kings Heath, 15th May 1967.

Kingston Row, off Cambridge Street, Civic Centre, May 1967.

Highfield Place/Granville Place, Anderton Street, Ladywood, 9th June 1967.

Jill Knight, MP for Edgbaston (second left), presents awards to the Four Oaks Musical Comedy Society, in the Midland Festival of Musical Theatre, Sutton Coldfield Town Hall, 19th June 1967.

Jeremy Child, Jean Shrimpton and Paul Jones filming a scene for "Privilege", Grand Hotel, 23rd June 1967. Most of the film was shot in the city.

Queens Road/Church Lane, Aston, June 1967.

Alma Street, Newtown, 11th July 1967.

Orchard Road/Belgrave Road, Balsall Heath, 4th September 1967.

Rear of Lawrence Street, Gosta Green, 8th September 1967.

The Green, Kings Norton, 11th October 1967.

Children mourning the loss of their bonfire, deliberately fired by Council Parks' employees a week earlier, Hazeldene Road, Sheldon, 28th October 1967. Officials said it was dangerously near to a hut.

Bull Ring shopping, 16th December 1967.

1968

Englehard Industries Ltd. (refiners) Vyse Street, Jewellery Quarter, 1968.

Craelius Co. Ltd. (diamond core and concrete drilling manufacturers and contractors), Rock Spring Works, Cheston Road, Aston, 4th January 1968.

A tranquil scene in St Philip's churchyard, as the Right Rev George Sinker, Provost and Assistant Bishop of Birmingham, picnics with children from Meadway Infants' School, Kitts Green, 9th July 1968.

Guild Council members, The University of Birmingham, 1968.

Patients sent by the Birmingham Hospital Saturday Fund to Kewstoke Convalescent Home, Summer 1968.

Male patients recuperate at Montrosa Convalescent Home, Weston-Super-Mare, Summer 1968.

Tyseley Railway Museum, c 1968.

An order, for the Pakistan Air Force, for a universal test rig for gas turbine fuel systems, is about to leave Birmingham Airport, 1968.

The new Palm House at the Botanical Gardens, Edgbaston, 7th August 1968.

Deputy Lord Mayor, Alderman James Meadows, sits astride Grey Sky, a police horse from Ladywood, at the Police, Fire and Ambulance Exhibition, Bull Ring Centre, 28th August 1968.

Skipper, Alan Smith, is held aloft after Warwickshire win the Gillette Cup (beating Sussex in the final), 7th September 1968.

Preparing to leave the stables for duty at St Andrew's football ground, Duke Street, 4th October 1968.

Touring the Bull Ring open-air market the Lord Mayor, Alderman Charles Simpson, enjoys a joke with the Lady Mayoress, 14th November 1968.

1969

Guests and members of the Federation of Master Builders pose with the Lord Mayor and Lady Mayoress,
Alderman and Mrs Charles Simpson, at the annual dinner/dance, Grand Hotel, Colmore Row,
10th January 1969.

Petitioning to draw attention to grievances over school discipline, Yardley Grammar School,
15th January 1969.

The newly-created Park Rangers prepare to start work for Birmingham Parks' Department. Tally Ho Police Training Centre, Edgbaston, 1969.

Grove Lane, Handsworth, c 1969.

Telephonists demand a fair deal, Bull Ring, 30th January 1969. This followed a protest meeting held at Digbeth Civic Hall.

Air Marshall Sir Andrew Humphrey inspects the guard of honour at Castle Vale Comprehensive School, 27th February 1969.

The Chief Constable of Birmingham, Sir Derrick Capper, with award winners in the Midlands' Crime Cut Campaign, Post and Mail House, 30th April 1969.

Trinity Terrace/Bedford Road, Camp Hill, 1969.

City Transport officials meet passengers complaining about the amalgamation of two bus stops above Perry Barr underpass, 5th November 1969.

97

Temple Row, 1969.

At a reception for overseas students, organised
by the Birmingham International Council, the
Lord Mayor, Alderman Neville Bosworth,
watches a demonstration of a classical dance
of southern India, Council House,
7th November 1969.

The Prime Minister, Harold Wilson, presents local girl
Ann Jones, with the 1969 Sportswoman of the Year award.

Court Road/Edward Road, Balsall Heath, 1969.

Rehearsals for the panto, "Babes in the Wood", Hippodrome, 21st December 1969. The robbers were played by Bernie Winters (centre) and his brother Mike (right).

Back Cover: Albany Hotel interior (top)

Film star, Clint Eastwood and his wife Maggie, relax on the terrace of the Albany Hotel, Smallbrook Ringway, 5th June 1967. After a short break in the city he flew to New Mexico to begin filming, "Hang 'Em High".

ACKNOWLEDGEMENTS

(for providing photographs, encouragement and numerous other favours)

Keith Ackrill; Neal and Joan Allen; Norman Bailey; Alan Bentley; The Birmingham City Council Dept. of Planning and Architecture; The Birmingham Post and Mail Ltd.; Denis and Rosie Brown; Anne Cannell; Eric and Mavis Hall; Patricia Harvey; Doug Hobson; Monty and Babs Jenkinson; Mavis Johnson; Dave, Thelma and Tom Jones; Diane Jones; Stanley Lamb; Joyce Lockwood; Arnold Manley; Sylvia Manton; Dennis Moore; George Peace; Jenny Scott; Keith Shakespeare; Brian and Freda Williams, Ken Windsor.

Please forgive any possible omissions. Every effort has been made to include all organisations and individuals involved in the book.

Residents demand better living conditions, Hingeston Street, Hockley, 2nd May 1969.